SUSAN STEGGALL is the author and illustrator of five other books
for Frances Lincoln: *On the Road* ("Hugely attractive . . . a beautiful
and satisfying conclusion." – *Guardian*), *The Life of a Car*
("Splendid . . . bursting with colour." – *Books for Keeps*),
Rattle and Rap ("An outstanding picture book." – *Inís*),
Busy Boats ("Every page has the interest and detail likely to
get young children thinking and talking." – *Books for Keeps*)
and *Red Car, Red Bus* ("Sure to be a big hit
with the very young" *IBBY Link*).

She trained as a designer before becoming a teacher
and was inspired to write about and illustrate cars, trains,
boats and buses by her two boys. All of her illustrations
are intricate collages made from many different sorts
of manufactured and handmade papers.
She lives in Hampshire, England.

For Ed

Text and illustrations copyright © Susan Steggall 2012
The right of Susan Steggall to be identified as the author and
illustrator of this work has been asserted by her in accordance with
the Copyright, Designs and Patents Act, 1988 (United Kingdom).

First published in Great Britain in 2012 and in the USA in 2013
by Frances Lincoln Children's Books,
74-77 White Lion Street, London, N1 9PF
www.franceslincoln.com

First paperback published in Great Britain in 2013

A catalogue record for this book is available from the British Library.

ISBN 978-1-84780-468-6

Illustrated with collages of torn paper

Printed in China

1 3 5 7 9 8 6 4 2

THE
DIGGERS
ARE
COMING!

Susan Steggall

F

FRANCES LINCOLN
CHILDREN'S BOOKS

and passing pieces of paper about.

They`re measuring up
and they`re marking out,

They *shave*
and s h i f t
and **shove** all day,

scraping soil
and stones away.

The diggers are coming!
The diggers are coming,

with **MASSIVE** metal mouths.

Their teeth are tearing at the ground and their tracks trudge round and round and round

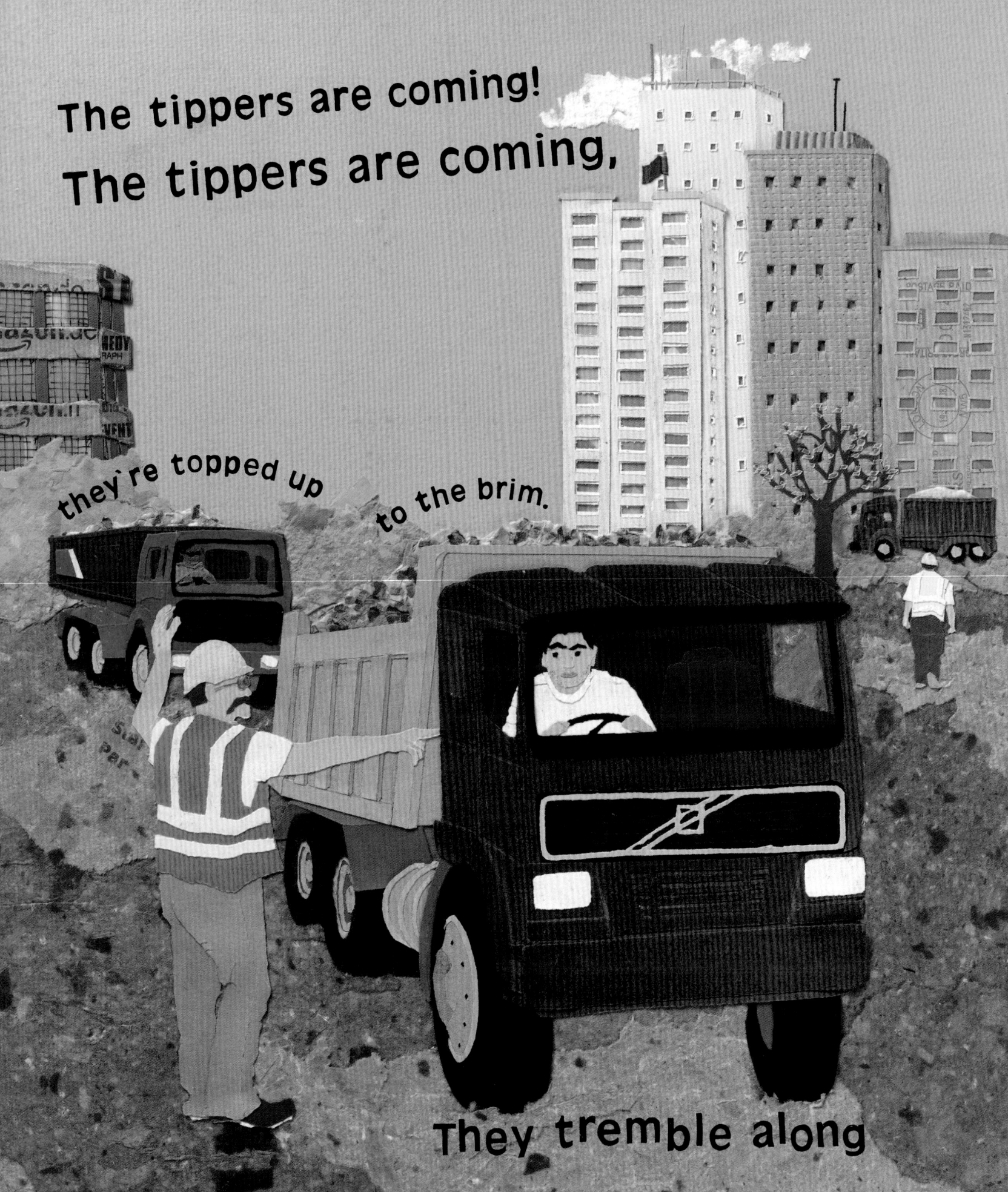

The mixers are coming!
The mixers are coming,

they tumble and twist and turn,

churning concrete round and round,
to dollop down into the ground.

They **beep** as they back up to let off their load,

then **THUNDER** away along the road.

The builders are coming!
The builders are coming,

with hard hats
and hammers and hods.

They're biffing
and bashing

The cranes are coming!
The cranes are coming,

with jibs and jacks
and booms.

They heave **HUGE** hefty hulks

up high

and hold
them
hanging
in the sky.

and steadily squash
all the bumpy bits out.

The vans are coming!
The vans are coming,

with cupboards
and chairs and chests.

They've *hurtled*
halfway through
the town.

They`re *stacked*
with stuff,
but it`s well strapped down.

The people are coming! The people are coming, with boxes and bundles and bags.

They`re moving in, and today`s the day!
Everything`s done and they`re here to stay.

MORE SUSAN STEGGALL TITLES
FROM FRANCES LINCOLN CHILDREN'S BOOKS

RATTLE AND RAP

Take the train to the seaside and join in as it whooshes through a tunnel, rattles across a level crossing and rumbles along the track, taking its passengers safely to their station.

THE LIFE OF A CAR

Follow the life of a car from when it leaves the factory, to being sold, driven, cleaned, crashed, scrapped and recycled. Featuring a glorious assortment of vehicles and big machines, this is the perfect book for all car and truck-loving readers.

ON THE ROAD

Follow a family as they drive past the garage, under the bridge and through the tunnel. With all sorts of vehicles, including a digger and a road sweeper, this simple story is perfect for even the youngest child.

BUSY BOATS

Follow a fishing boat that leaves port in the morning and returns in the afternoon. From freighters being loaded with cargo, lifeboats, a ferry, speed boats, rowing boats and yachts, to an ocean liner, this is a book that celebrates the variety and beauty of boats and ships of every kind.

RED CAR, RED BUS

This beautifully simple picture book introduces the concept of patterns to the youngest child. With an ever-growing traffic queue and entertaining background storylines, this highly original book is ideal for young readers.

Frances Lincoln titles are available from all good bookshops.
You can also buy books and find out more about your favourite titles,
authors and illustrators on our website: www.franceslincoln.com